The American Mosaic
Immigration Today

Undocumented Immigrants

Sara Howell

PowerKiDS press.

New York

Published in 2015 by The Rosen Publishing Group, Inc.
29 East 21st Street, New York, NY 10010

First Edition

Editors: Jennifer Way and Norman D. Graubart
Book Design: Andrew Povolny
Photo Research: Katie Stryker

Photo Credits: Cover Chris Kleponis/AFP/Getty Images; p. 5 Bloomberg/ Getty Images; p. 6 Jack Hollingsworth/Digital Vision/Getty Images; p. 7 Andreas Rodriguez/iStock/Thinkstock; p. 8 Phototreat/iStock/ Thinkstock; p. 9 romakoma/Shutterstock.com; p. 10 Jeffrey M. Frank/ Shutterstock.com; p. 11 bikeriderlondon/Shutterstock.com; pp. 12, 16 Chip Somodevilla/Getty Images; p. 13 Blend Images - Hill Street Studios/ Brand X Pictures/Getty Images; p. 14 fotostorm/E+/Getty Images; p. 15 Ariel Skelley/Blend Images/Getty Images; p. 17 Nick Mattiuzzo/iStock/ Thinkstock; p. 19 moodboard/Vetta/Getty Images; p. 20 tpnagasima/ iStock/Thinkstock; p. 21 Brendan Smialowski/AFP/Getty Images; p. 22 Michael Bezjian/WireImage/Getty Images.

Library of Congress Cataloging-in-Publication Data

Howell, Sara.
Undocumented immigrants / by Sara Howell. — First Edition.
    pages cm. — (The American mosaic : immigration today)
Includes index.
ISBN 978-1-4777-6744-3 (library binding) — ISBN 978-1-4777-6745-0 (pbk.) — ISBN 978-1-4777-6650-7 (6-pack)
1. Illegal aliens—United States—Juvenile literature. 2. United States— Emigration and immigration—Juvenile literature. I. Title.
JV6483.H683 2015
364.1'370973—dc23
                                    2014002353

Manufactured in the United States of America

CPSIA Compliance Information: Batch #WS14PK1: For Further Information contact Rosen Publishing, New York, New York at 1-800-237-9932

Contents

Each year, more than one million people move to the United States. They may move for work, to be closer to family, or for other reasons. People who move from one country to another are called **immigrants**.

Most immigrants who come to the United States have permission to live and work here. However, some immigrants live and work in the United States even though they do not have **documents** that allow them to live here. These people are called undocumented immigrants. Some people use the word "illegal" to describe them. The act of immigration can be illegal, but no person can be illegal.

Jose Antonio Vargas gives speeches about immigration. born in the Philippines and brought to the United State was 12 years old. He is an undocumented immigrant.

California and Texas used to be part of Mexico. Mexican culture is a big part of these states' cultures.

Today, there are about 40 million foreign-born people living in the United States. About 11.7 million of those people are undocumented immigrants. About 2.5 million undocumented immigrants live in California. That is more than any other state. Most undocumented immigrants come to the United States from Mexico.

Dangerous Crossing

Some parts of the border do not have a fence. These parts can still be very difficult to cross because the desert is so hot.

Coming to the United States illegally can be dangerous. The border between the United States and Mexico is in the Southwest. This desert area is hot and has little water. Each year about 200 undocumented immigrants die crossing the border. Most die from **dehydration**, or not having enough water in the body.

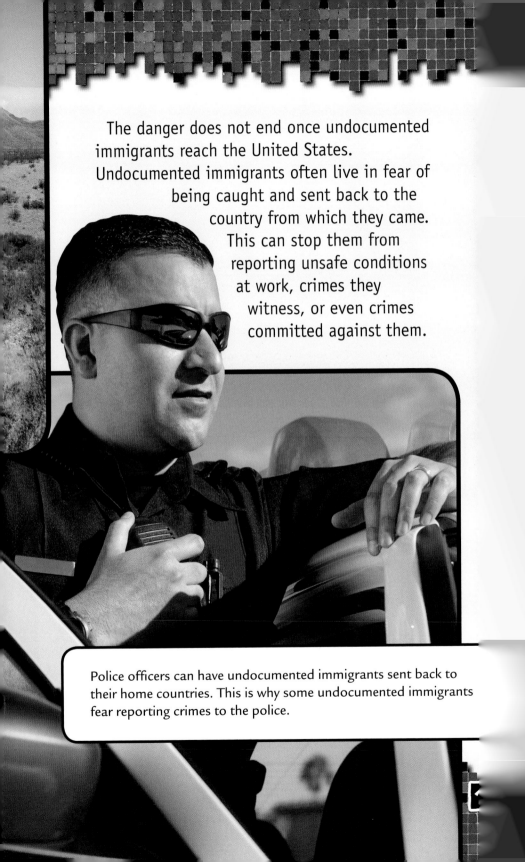

The danger does not end once undocumented immigrants reach the United States. Undocumented immigrants often live in fear of being caught and sent back to the country from which they came. This can stop them from reporting unsafe conditions at work, crimes they witness, or even crimes committed against them.

Police officers can have undocumented immigrants sent back to their home countries. This is why some undocumented immigrants fear reporting crimes to the police.

Immigrants' Rights

This is the original signed copy of the US Constitution, at the National Archives in Washington, DC. This document is the basis for Americans' rights.

All people who live in the United States, both **citizens** and immigrants, have certain rights. A right is something that people must be allowed to do. Many of these rights are listed in the US **Constitution**.

Undocumented immigrants have the right to the same treatment from the police and the courts as everyone else. Those under 18 have the right to a free public education.

The laws of the United States also protect undocumented immigrants. This means that no one is allowed to hurt them or steal from them just because they are in the country illegally.

POLLING PLACE
投票站　CASILLA ELECTORAL
投票所　LUGAR NG BOTOHAN
투표소　PHÒNG PHIẾU

American citizens can vote, but undocumented immigrants cannot.

Making an Impact

Undocumented immigrants have an important impact on the US **economy**. As do others in the United States, they pay **taxes** to the US government. The government then uses these taxes to pay for schools, fire departments, highways, and many other things. Undocumented immigrants pay sales tax each time they buy something. They pay property taxes if they own a home. About 75 percent pay taxes on the money they earn at their jobs.

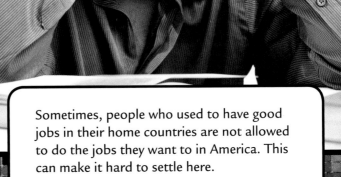

Sometimes, people who used to have good jobs in their home countries are not allowed to do the jobs they want to in America. This can make it hard to settle here.

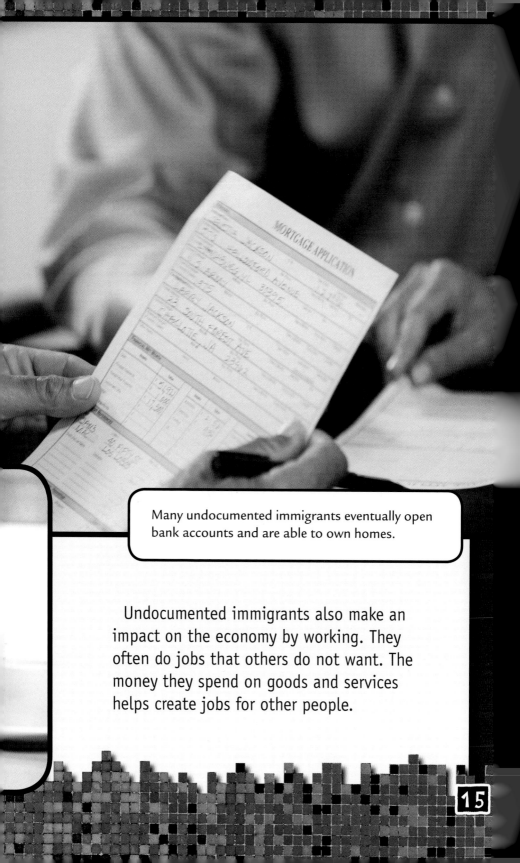

Many undocumented immigrants eventually open bank accounts and are able to own homes.

Undocumented immigrants also make an impact on the economy by working. They often do jobs that others do not want. The money they spend on goods and services helps create jobs for other people.

mmigration Laws

In the United States, the federal government makes laws that apply to everyone in the country. Other laws are made by state and local governments and apply only to those in a certain area. Because of this, laws affecting undocumented immigrants can be very different in different places.

In the case *Arizona v. United States*, the US Supreme Court decided that local police couldn't enforce national immigration laws.

Portland, Maine, is a sanctuary city.

Some states, such as those near the US-Mexico border, have more undocumented immigrants than others. One state, Arizona, has passed laws making it harder for undocumented immigrants to live there. Some cities, such as El Paso, Texas, call themselves **sanctuary** cities. There, police are not allowed to ask about a person's immigration **status**.

Deportation

Undocumented immigrants often try to avoid dealing with the police or the US government. This is because such immigrants are breaking immigration laws by being here. If they are caught, they might be sent out of the country. This is called **deportation**.

First, the undocumented immigrant is given a notice to appear at a deportation hearing. At the hearing, an immigration judge will look at the evidence and decide if the person has immigrated illegally. If so, US Immigration and Customs Enforcement, or ICE, will remove the immigrant from the country.

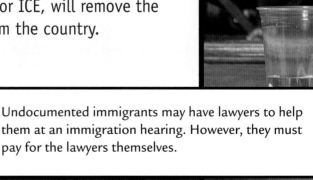

Undocumented immigrants may have lawyers to help them at an immigration hearing. However, they must pay for the lawyers themselves.

Finding a Path to Citizenship

Many undocumented immigrants hope to become US citizens. Today, there are very few ways that is possible. Adults who marry US citizens may apply to become **permanent residents**. However, there are many rules that make this difficult.

Getting any kind of visa can be difficult if you have entered the United States illegally.

Former secretary of homeland security Janet Napolitano carried out DACA. DACA keeps people brought to the United States as children from being deported.

Some in the US government have suggested ways to help immigrants brought into the country as children. In 2012, the Deferred Action for Childhood Arrivals, or DACA, was announced. Another suggestion, the DREAM Act, would make it easier for these immigrants to find jobs, go to college, and become legal residents. However, it has not been passed into law.

The American Mosaic

The United States is sometimes called a melting pot. This is because people from many different backgrounds have come together to create one society. We can also think of the country as a **mosaic**. A mosaic is a picture made by fitting many small pieces together to create a larger work.

No matter their status or how they got here, immigrants have left their mark on American music, art, food, and language. In this way, the culture of the United States is always growing and changing!

Cesar Millan, star of the TV show *Dog Whisperer with Cesar Millan*, was born in Mexico. He was an undocumented immigrant until 2000. He is now a citizen.

Glossary

citizens (SIH-tih-zenz) People who were born in or have a right to live in a country.

Constitution (kon-stih-TOO-shun) The basic rules by which the United States is governed.

dehydration (dee-hy-DRAY-shun) The state of having lost too much water.

deportation (dee-por-TAY-shun) The act of being sent out of a country.

documents (DOK-yoo-ments) Written or printed statements that give official information about something.

economy (ih-KAH-nuh-mee) The way in which a country or a business oversees its goods and services.

immigrants (IH-muh-grunts) People who move to a new country from another country.

mosaic (moh-ZAY-ik) A picture made by fitting together small pieces of stone, glass, or tile and pasting them in place.

permanent residents (PER-muh-nint REH-zih-dents) People who are not citizens but who have the right to live and work in a country forever.

quota (KWOH-tuh) The number or part of a share that is assigned to a certain group.

sanctuary (SANK-choo-weh-ree) A place where people are kept safe.

sponsor (SPON-ser) To take on responsibility for.

status (STA-tus) Someone's position compared to others.

taxes (TAKS-ez) Money added to the price of something or paid to a government for community services.

visa (VEE-zuh) Official permission to enter a country.

Index

Websites

Due to the changing nature of Internet links, PowerKids Press has developed an online list of websites related to the subject of this book. This site is updated regularly. Please use this link to access the list:

www.powerkidslinks.com/mosa/undoc/